APR 2000

Ecosystems of North America

The Deserts of the Southwest

Maria Mudd Ruth

Benchmark Books

MARSHALL CAVENDISH
NEW YORK

Series Consultant: Stephen R. Kellert, Ph.D., School of Forestry and Environmental Studies, Yale University

Consultant: Richard Haley, Director, Goodwin Conservation Center

Benchmark Books
Marshall Cavendish Corporation
99 White Plains Road
Tarrytown, New York 10591-9001

Library of Congress Cataloging-in-Publication Data

Mudd Ruth, Maria.
       The deserts of the Southwest / Maria Mudd Ruth.
             p.   cm.—(Ecosystems of North America)
       Includes bibliographical references (p.   ) and index.
       Summary: Examines the deserts of the Southwest, their ecosystems, and their responses to
temperature and weather.
       ISBN 0-7614-0899-1 (lib. bdg.)
       1. Deserts—Southwest, New—Juvenile literature. [1. Deserts—Southwest, New. 2. Desert ecology.
3. Ecology.] I. Title. II. Series.
GB616.S67M83   1999   97-49842
577.54'0974—dc21   CIP
                                                            AC

Photo Credits

The photographs in this book are used by permission and through the courtesy of:
Animals Animals/Earth Scenes: Richard Day 18; Paul Freed 31; C. C. Lockwood 35;
Paul A. Berquist 36, 51; Mark A. Chappell 37; Thane 38-39; John Gerlach 42; L.L.T. Rhodes 45, 55;
Phyllis Greenberg 44; S. Michael Bisceglie 53; Mickey Gibson 56-57; Doug Wechsler back cover.
Photo Researchers: Merlin D. Tuttle 20; Stephen Krasemann 22; Michael Hubrich 29; George Ranalli
32-33; Jim Corwin 46-47. *Timeframe Photography Inc.:* Charles D. Winters 27. *Tom Stack &
Associates:* Tom Algire front cover, 4-5; G. C. Kelley 9; Brian Parker 14-15; Joe McDonald 17; John
Shaw 24-25; Doug Sokell 59; Thomas Kitchin 52; Jeff Foott 49. Cover design by Ann Antoshak for BBI.

Series Created and Produced by BOOK BUILDERS INCORPORATED

Printed in Hong Kong
65432

Contents

Land of Extremes

Deserts are found on every continent and cover one-seventh of the land on Earth. In North America, the desert spreads across the southwestern United States and south into Mexico. In the United States, the Southwest deserts include parts of Oregon, Idaho, Nevada, Utah, Colorado, Wyoming, New Mexico, Arizona, and California. They are nearly enclosed by a series of towering mountain ranges: the Cascades, the Sierra Nevada, the Rockies, and the Sierra Madre.

Before we explore this vast expanse of desert up close, let's take a look at the desert from a point high above the earth. As you look down, you can clearly see the fortress-like mountain ranges. The desert that lies inside them is not all sand dunes as you may have imagined. Lots of land is empty, flat, and beige. Rising out of the flat land you see massive, rust-colored rock formations shaped like arches, chimneys, pipe organs, columns, and castles. In some places, dark boulders are scattered evenly across hundreds of miles. Mountains are everywhere, jutting up like peaks of frosting on top of a cake. You sight deep valleys, wind-sculpted canyons,

Although rainfall is scarce, life is abundant in the Southwest deserts.

frost-covered plateaus, and sand dunes that look like frozen waves. Surprisingly, there are wide rivers, lakes, and lush oases. And everywhere you see signs of life: small forests of tree-sized cactuses, low-growing shrubs, fields of brilliantly colored flowers, a small herd of deer, a lone hawk, even sprawling cities and small towns.

How can all this be called a desert? The North American desert is much more than sand dunes and cactuses. Water, wind, and weather have eroded and shaped the land over millions of years. Differences in elevation, rainfall, and temperature have influenced the species, or kinds, of plants and animals that live here. These variations have created five main deserts: the Great Basin, the Colorado Plateau, the Mojave, the Sonoran, and the Chihuahuan. The northernmost desert, the Great Basin, which is called a cold desert, receives most of its precipitation as snow. The other three deserts are hot deserts, which get their precipitation as rain. The precipitation in these deserts falls at different times of year and in a variety of ways. But all of the regions have one thing in common: they are extremely dry.

Most scientists define a desert as a place that receives less than 10 inches (25 cm) of precipitation a year. [By comparison, New York City gets about 45 inches (114 cm) annually.] North American deserts are dry because of their location on the dry side of the mountain ranges that surround them. As moist air from the Pacific Ocean and Gulf Coast is forced to rise over these mountains, it cools down. Clouds form and rain or snow falls on the upwind side of the mountains. By the time the air reaches the leeward, or downwind, side of the mountain, its moisture is depleted. Deserts created in this way are called rain shadow deserts.

North American deserts cannot even count on 10 inches of precipitation in a year. Most places get between 4 and 8 inches (20 cm). In some places it may not rain for twelve months at a stretch. When the rain does come, it might be in the form of a cloudburst so violent that it causes flash floods. The rain might also come as a light sprinkle, almost too little to notice. Either way, most of the precipitation in the desert is quickly evaporated, or turned into

The Deserts of the Southwest

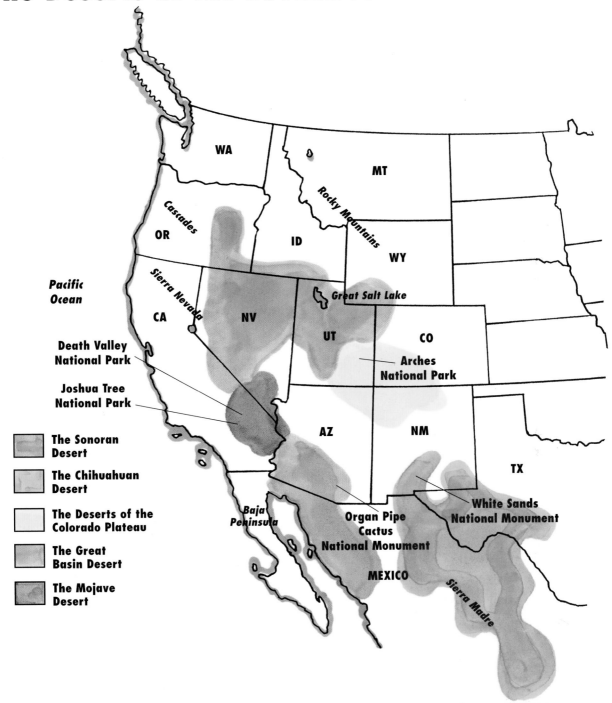

Death Valley National Park

Joshua Tree National Park

Arches National Park

Organ Pipe Cactus National Monument

White Sands National Monument

The Sonoran Desert

The Chihuahuan Desert

The Deserts of the Colorado Plateau

The Great Basin Desert

The Mojave Desert

Several distinct regions are found within the deserts of the Southwest, which include some 500,000 square miles (1.3 million sq km) in the United States and Mexico.

tiny droplets of water called **vapor** by the sun, wind, and dry air. This means that very little water is available to plants and animals. And what little water they can get is difficult to keep. Evaporation robs moisture from every living thing exposed in the desert.

The desert is also a place of extreme temperatures. In the summer, temperatures often reach well over 100 degrees Fahrenheit (38° C). At night, the desert cools down quickly, with the temperatures often plunging close to freezing. Few plants can survive these harsh conditions. This leads to more problems: erosion and poor soil. Without a mat of vegetation, the soil is fully exposed to the sun, wind, and flooding rains. **Organic matter**, which is made up of decayed plants and animals and provides nutrients to the soil, is quickly dried out and blown or washed away. And in a flash flood, tons of soil can be washed away in a matter of hours as storm water rushes down desert hillsides.

It Takes a Community

So how can anything live in the desert? For most life forms, this **habitat**—the place that has all of the things an organism needs to live—is too harsh, making survival impossible. But an amazing number and variety of plants and animals do live here. In fascinating, unique, and often mind-boggling ways, the plants and animals of the desert have developed **adaptations**, or special features and tricks, that help them cope with the harsh conditions. Some species even thrive in the desert world. Let's take a closer look at some of these survivors.

Imagine you are walking through that flat, beige desert land. Your mouth is dry and your throat is parched. The sun is scorching you, and the air has dried the sweat from your skin. Your canteen of water is nearly empty. You kick at a few small rocks scattered on top of the crusty soil. You take a last big sip of water from your canteen. You wander over a small hill and spot a group of giant saguaro cactuses. Each is about 40 feet (12 m) tall with several large branches that look like raised arms. You move closer. The cactuses are covered in clusters of long spines. You step back. Then you see a woodpecker flying toward one of the cactuses and disappearing

An elf owl finds shelter from the heat and protection from predators inside a giant saguaro cactus.

into the trunk. Moving closer, you see a small hole from which you hear the chirping of baby birds. You notice that most of the cactuses here have holes in them. From one hole a small owl peeks out. Suddenly a mouse scampers up another cactus with a seed in its mouth. It slips into a hole with straw sticking out of it. On the side of the cactus, you also see clusters of white waxy flowers. Perched on top of one blossom is a small bird that pokes its head into the flower to sip nectar.

Reminded of your thirst, you start walking back to your campsite for more water. You begin to wonder about the connections among the plants and animals you've just seen. Where do they get their water? Why do they all live together? Why is the cactus so huge and spiny? How can birds live inside a cactus? What does the owl eat?

Many of these questions can be answered by a kind of scientist called an **ecologist.** Ecology is the study of the relationships among different species of plants and animals in their surroundings, or

environment. The environment of a cactus, for instance, includes the amount of sunlight and rain it receives, the temperature of the air around it, the soil it grows in, the minerals in the soil and plants growing near it, the animals that eat it, and the insects and animals that pollinate it. To make survival in the desert easier, different species of animals and plants learn to interact, forming **biological communities.** People live in communities of families, neighborhoods, villages, cities, and towns for much the same reasons. Within the Southwest deserts, there are many biological communities—some are made up of many different species, others of just a few. In the desert, communities form where water is likely to be available. The desert **ecosystem** is made up of all of these biological communities together with their environment.

Every Drop Counts

Water is the most precious resource in the desert. While the lack of water defines the desert, it is the presence of water that determines how and where different species live and what their community is like.

Water flows through all living things. The endless movement of water between the atmosphere and the land is called the **water cycle.** Let's begin our desert water cycle with some much needed rain. The rain falls from the clouds onto the land. Here, it may soak into the soil or sand or collect in bodies of water, such as lakes, streams, or small pools. Some water passes through living things: plants soak up water through their roots, and animals consume water by drinking and by eating plants or other animals. Some water is returned to the environment when animals release body heat or get rid of their body wastes. All of this liquid water, no matter where it falls or how it is consumed, is evaporated. In North American deserts, between 70 and 160 inches (1.8–4 m) of water is lost each year through evaporation. This vapor is carried up by rising warm air. When the water vapor reaches the high, cool air, it condenses and turns into larger water droplets that form clouds. Eventually, the water falls again as rain, and the water cycle begins again.

In the desert, water is the rarest necessity. Organisms must have adaptations for getting water and for losing as little water as possible.

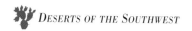

Sunlight Becomes You

The water cycle alone cannot maintain life in the desert. Living things must trap energy from the sun. They use it for growth or warmth or movement, and then release it. To follow a tiny trickle of this great flow of energy, start with sunlight on a cactus. The cactus traps light energy through its skin and spines and uses it to make sugars by the process called **photosynthesis.** These sugars are stored in the cactus's fruits or seeds. A squirrel that eats the fruit uses part of the energy for growing and part of it as fuel for scampering around the desert. The squirrel also loses some of the energy in the form of heat and droppings. Insects and bacteria take a share of energy from the droppings. A hawk will get a share of the energy if it can catch and eat the squirrel. Sooner or later, all the trapped energy stored in the squirrel is used as fuel for another organism. It is then released as heat into the environment, where it is finally lost. No organism can get it back.

In this energy story, the plant is a **producer** because it uses energy from the sun to produce sugars that animals can use as food. The squirrel is a plant eater, or **primary consumer.** And the hawk, which hunts and kills other organisms for food, is a **predator,** or **secondary consumer.** Bacteria, fungi, insects, and other organisms that break down wastes and dead matter are called **decomposers.**

Energy flows through a **food chain.** This pathway describes feeding relationships in which one species is eaten by another species that is, in turn, eaten by a larger species. For example, grasshoppers feed on the leaves of a creosote bush, and grasshopper mice eat the grasshoppers. A kit fox catches and eats the mice. The last eater, the kit fox in this particular chain, is at the top of the food chain.

Different species may be involved in more than one food chain. Small birds might also eat the grasshoppers, competing with the mice for food. Owls and hawks compete with the foxes for a share of the mice to feed their young. Different food chains often intercon-nect to form a large network called a **food web.**

To know the desert well, we need to learn about the different seasons and how they affect the behavior of the plants and animals that live here. When does it rain? What happens to plants and animals when it rains? How long does the dry season last? What effect do wind and snow have? It helps to learn something about the daily rhythms of the desert—the changes in light and temperature over the course of the day and night.

The Southwest desert is a mosaic of many different deserts. Within the five main deserts, there is a great variety of climate, elevation, soil, and plant and animal life. The northern Mojave Desert, for example, looks very different from the southern part. And within the northern part, there are snow-capped mountains as well as dry, flat valleys. In one valley, there are species of plants and animals that do not exist anywhere else.

We will explore the Southwest desert by looking at some of the pieces of the mosaic. These pieces are distinct geographic features: the bajada, dune, canyon, basin, salt lake, valley, and oasis. Water has shaped these features in different ways. Rain that falls in the canyon does not behave in the same way as it does in the basin. The climate and precipitation patterns differ. The basin gets a one-season blast of snow, the bajada gets two seasons of rainfall. Each supports distinct communities of plants and animals. Plants found growing in the dune are not found in the oasis; animals that have adapted to the bajada do not live in the valley.

Our exploration of these environments will include the plant and animal communities as well as the human ones. Millions of people live in the desert—in cities and towns, in near-wilderness and on reservations. Many people visit the desert for vacation to enjoy its natural beauty and its warm, dry climate. Others work in the desert, on farms and ranches and in mineral mining companies. We will look at the impact of humans on the desert. Whether we live in the desert or are just visiting, we have an enormous effect upon the desert ecosystem, just as it, in turn, affects us.

Survival Skills

It is raining in the Sonoran Desert. The windshield wipers are on full speed. Maybe you'll be able to see a few cactuses out the car window when the rain lets up. You imagine your first excursion into the desert will be disappointing—barren terrain, gray skies, and rain. You park the car and put on your boots and raincoat. But as you step out of the car, the rain stops. The clouds disappear over the mountains, revealing a bright blue sky and a landscape glistening and sparkling in the bright sunshine. You toss your raincoat back in the car and begin to walk.

Much to your surprise the hillsides are blanketed with flowers—gold poppies, blue lupine, pink owl clover, and bright yellow clumps of brittlebush. Small green leaves cover every branch of the creosote bushes, ocotillos, and mesquite trees. There are cactuses of every shape and size: squat barrels, huge columns, pin cushions, pancakes, and old-fashioned organ pipes. Many of them are tipped with delicate blossoms of pink, peach, white, and yellow.

These are the colors of springtime in the Sonoran Desert. This hot desert straddles Mexico and the United States. It covers parts of California and Arizona and includes mountains, river valleys, beaches, sand

In the Sonoran Desert, the gently sloping bajadas and two seasons of rain create an ideal environment for desert blooms.

dunes, lava fields, and craters from ancient volcanoes. Taken as a whole, the Sonoran has the hottest temperatures of the Southwest deserts. But it has two rainy seasons—summer is filled with storms, and winter with showers. This pattern of biseasonal rainfall occurs in no other desert.

Most of the biological communities are found in the **bajadas**, gently sloping hills made of gravel, sand, and silt washed down from the surrounding mountains. The soil of the bajadas holds more moisture than other landforms, such as steep mountainsides or rocky cliffs. The bajadas and the rainfall create a desert of great **biodiversity**, or number of species. Within the Sonoran, there are 2,500 species of plants, including 300 species of cactuses and more than 100 different species of animals. This doesn't seem like the desert at all—until the drought sets in. From April through June the rain is barely measurable. Daytime temperatures heat up to 100 degrees Fahrenheit (38° C) in May, then stay there until September. Summer storms bring another four inches (10 cm) of rain. Then comes more drought until the winter showers. How do so many plants and animals survive in this feast-or-famine desert?

During a 1991 highway construction project in Phoenix, Arizona, the skeletal remains of 800 people from the ancient Hohokam Indian tribe were found. They lived between A.D. 300 and 1450 in the Sonoran Desert, where they engineered complex irrigation canals.

Secret Strategies of Plants

One of the best places to find the answers is at the Organ Pipe Cactus National Monument in Arizona. This 515-square-mile (1,335-sq-km) preserve is part of the National Park System. Plants and animals live in near-wilderness conditions, making it an ideal place to study survival strategies. Deserts feature two kinds of plants: annuals and perennials. **Annual** plants cannot withstand the seasons of drought and heat in the desert. They complete their entire life cycle in a short time, usually within one season. **Perennial** plants can withstand all seasons throughout many years.

Annuals sprout in the spring when it is cool and wet, then quickly grow, bloom, and produce seeds. Just weeks after blooming,

Delicate Mexican gold poppies bloom in the spring and then produce drought-resistant seeds that can survive the dry seasons.

as soon as the heat and drought announce the end of spring, they wither and vanish. The leaves, stems, and roots of annuals have no special adaptations to withstand drought. But their seeds do. The seeds of the Mexican gold poppy are coated in a special chemical that prevents them from drying out. This coating must be washed off by the Sonoran's heavy winter rains before the poppy seeds will sprout again. If winter rains are not heavy enough, poppy seeds can remain dormant for several years. When the rains are right, the poppy will burst forth again in a dazzling blaze of color.

Desert blossoms attract a bevy of insects and small animals that come to to feed on the sweet liquid called nectar inside the flowers. As the animals drink, they are also being covered with pollen and are bringing it from plant to plant. When a bee is fed, a flower is pollinated. When millions of flowers carpet the bajadas, the competition for a pollinator is fierce. The flowers that bloom in the daytime are pollinated mostly by animals that are **diurnal**, or active during the day. Some plants avoid the competition by blooming at night. These blossoms are visited by creatures that are **nocturnal**, or active during the night. Moths and bats are some of the busiest nighttime pollinators.

When the drought and heat of early summer begin in the desert, the annuals fade away, and the landscape belongs to plants with strategies for coping with extreme heat and drought. The cactus is king of the perennials. Like all cactuses, the organ pipe cactus uses several survival strategies at once. The organ pipe has thick, pulpy stems for storing water. These stems are pleated like an accordion. When it rains, they channel rainwater to the cactus's roots. When the roots soak up the water into the center of the cactus stems, the pleats expand so the cactus can hold more water. The cactus's thick skin is protected by a coating of wax that reduces

The organ pipe cactus is well adapted to the desert. Its pleated stems expand to hold as much water as possible when it rains and contract during the drought to expose as little skin as possible to the drying air and sun.

water loss through evaporation. Most plants lose water through their leaves, but cactuses have small spines instead of leaves. The process of photosynthesis, which occurs in the leaves of other plants, takes place in the green skin and inside the cactus's pithy core. Cactuses are armed with a variety of spines, including long sharp needles, sharp hairs, fish hooks, and barbs. These discourage rodents and other animals from trampling on these plants and from eating them. Organ pipe cactuses grow shallow roots that spread over a large area, so they can soak up as much water as possible. These roots release chemicals that are toxic to other plants and discourage them from rooting nearby.

When it rains, all parts of the cactus get involved. Spines trap the smallest drops of rain, which are funneled down the pleats and onto the plant roots. Roots soak up water from far and wide. An organ pipe cactus can guzzle as much as 40 gallons (151 l) in twenty-four hours. As the cactus swells with water, the pleats expand so the cactus's skin doesn't burst. Occasionally, cactuses do absorb too much too quickly. Their skin may split in places, or they may get too heavy for their root systems and crash to the desert floor. In most cases, though, they absorb and store only enough water to nourish them through the dry season.

Cactus Hotel

In every ecosystem, there is a species that has a large effect on many species in its community or ecosystem. This species is called a **keystone species**. In the Sonoran, a keystone species is the giant saguaro cactus—the symbol of the desert itself. These giants can grow to heights of 50 feet (15 m), weigh tons, and live for two hundred years. The saguaro provides shelter and food for a great variety of desert animals.

Let's start with the gila woodpecker, which makes its home in the saguaro. The woodpecker pecks a hole in a high spot on the trunk or branch and excavates a boot-sized cavity where it builds its nest. Here in this lofty spine-protected shelter, the woodpecker lays its eggs and raises its young, safe from snakes, rodents, and other predators who cannot climb up the spiny trunk. The thick walls of

Night-blooming plants are visited by nocturnal creatures, such as this bat, that sip the flower's nectar in the cool of the evening.

the cactus also provide the woodpecker protection from the broiling days and cold or freezing nights.

Each year the gila woodpecker abandons its nest for a new one. The saguaro is not empty for long. Pygmy owls, bluebirds, warblers, cactus wrens, woodrats, lizards, and other animals take refuge or nest in the spine-guarded holes. And what does the saguaro get in return for all this hospitality? The gila woodpecker and other residents help the saguaro by catching and eating various insects that would bring disease to the cactus. This kind of relationship between organisms in which both benefit is called **mutualistic**. In the desert, where resources such as food, water, and shelter are limited, mutualistic relationships are often necessary to the survival of both participants. The gila gets a protected, air-conditioned shelter, and the saguaro is less likely to be infested with disease-carrying insects.

In the cool of a spring evening, the saguaro opens its waxy white and yellow blossoms. These attract nocturnal creatures such as moths, who sip the nectar and pollinate the cactus. The blossoms and the moths attract long-tongued bats that sip nectar, eat the moths, and pollinate the cactus. Elf owls fly out of their saguaro nests to feast on scorpions and spiders that come out at night to hunt other insects. A snake attempts to slither its way up the cactus to

Design Your Own Drought-Resistant Leaf

Plants lose a great deal of water through their leaves by evaporation. In the desert, plants have evolved small leaves or spines instead of leaves to conserve moisture. This experiment shows how the rate of evaporation changes with different leaf shapes and structures. You will need:

- three paper towels
- a sheet of waxed paper (about the same size as the paper towel)
- two paper clips
- a cookie sheet or piece of aluminum foil (about 18 inches [46 cm] wide)

1. Dampen the three paper towels with water.

2. Lay one paper towel flat on the cookie sheet or foil.

3. Roll up the second paper towel and place it next to the first paper towel.

4. Roll the third paper towel. Roll the waxed paper around this paper towel. It will go around several times.

5. Close the ends of the waxed paper with the paper clips.

6. Place the third paper towel on the cookie sheet or foil.

7. Place the cookie sheet or foil in a sunny spot—indoors or outdoors.

8. After twenty-four hours, unroll the paper towels and feel the paper.

Like a large, flat leaf, the first paper towel dries out because it has more exposed surface area; water evaporates more quickly. Like the leaves of many desert plants, the second paper towel is thick and/or round to reduce the exposed surface area. Rolled like this, the paper towel conserves much—but not all—of its moisture. Like the paper towel covered in waxed paper, many desert plants are coated with a waxy substance that reduces water loss even more. Cactuses conserve nearly all of their moisture because they have small, needle-shaped "leaves" and are coated in wax.

Would the rate of evaporation increase or decrease if you put the two rolled paper towels in the shade? In front of a fan?

The kit fox, like many desert mammals, stays cool in its burrow by day, then emerges at night to hunt or forage for food.

eat the elf owl's unguarded eggs. Discouraged by the spines, the snake searches the ground for prey—perhaps the pack rat busily nibbling on the saguaro's juicy red fruit. The rat quickly scampers away, leaving half-eaten fruit for other animals. This hubbub lures the kit fox out of its den to hunt for prey—perhaps a rodent, a bird, or even a scorpion. The saguaro is an important link in several food chains and a center of activity for nocturnal animals. The saguaro is also an important food source, directly and indirectly.

When the saguaro dies, it gives life to other plants and animals. Its trunk and branches will provide new homes for scorpions, termites, and lizards. Over time, a variety of decomposer organisms will help turn the water and nutrients in the fallen giant back into soil.

The saguaro cactus has also played an important role for human communities living in the Sonoran Desert. The Papago have lived in the heart of the Sonoran Desert for centuries, planting corn, peppers, melons, and beans on land they irrigate and harvesting the sweet saguaro fruits. The fruit is eaten fresh, cooked to make jam, or dried. The juice is fermented for Papago rituals to bring summer rains. The saguaro fruit is still an important plant for the six thousand Papago living in the bountiful Sonoran.

Changes in the Sonoran

Following the Papago and other Indian nations, waves of explorers, missionaries, farmers, copper and silver miners, cattle ranchers, and settlers moved into the Sonoran. Many left their mark: abandoned mines, overgrazed land, and deserted buildings. In the early 1900s, settlers built dams to supply the small villages and farms with water. Some towns, such as Arizona's Tucson and Phoenix, grew into major cities. Water from the Colorado River is pumped from hundreds of miles away to meet the needs of the growing population. The dry land is watered and the hot desert air cooled by air conditioners. Grassy lawns, shade trees, swimming pools, and golf courses have sprung up among the houses, office buildings, shopping malls, and interstate highways.

During its lifetime, a saguaro cactus produces 40 million seeds. Only one is likely to survive to maturity.

This is not the only loss in the Sonoran Desert. In recent years, it has become fashionable for wealthy homeowners in the cities and suburbs of the Sonoran Desert to have one or two saguaro cactuses in their garden. A large cactus is expensive. Cactus thieves dig up hundreds of saguaros from the desert each year. Sadly, the saguaro has now joined the list of endangered plants. Today, saguaros are protected by law.

Remote areas of the Sonoran remain hot, dry, and untamable. Somewhere in between these two extremes are the wildlife refuges, military bases, Indian reservations, and national parks where we can still experience the beauty of the Sonoran Desert and learn about the effect humans have had on the many layers of life within this ecosystem.

Hidden Life

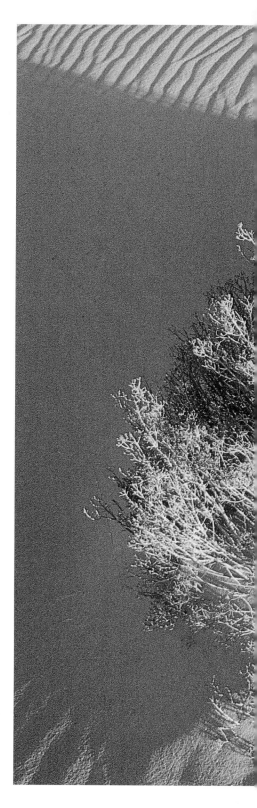

*T*he glare is intense. The pure whiteness of the landscape seems to double the brightness of the midday sun. Even with your sunglasses on and hat brim pulled way down, you need to squint to see. Before you lies a sea of giant white sand dunes that engulf the desert. They look like massive frozen waves, rising and falling for miles as they reach toward the distant mountains. The smallest dunes are about 20 feet high (6 m), the largest about 40 feet (12 m)—about as high as a three-story house. The wind kicks up, and wisps of sand blow up from the crests of the dunes. A hot breeze blows across your face, but you are not sweating in this dry air. Shimmering waves of heat rise from the dunes. You look toward the horizon again, half-expecting a caravan of camels to appear. But this is not the Sahara. This is the Chihuahuan Desert, the southernmost of the Southwest deserts.

The Chihuahuan Desert lies between two great mountain ranges in the isolated highlands of Mexico and in small portions of Texas and New Mexico. It is a desert of high plains, plateaus, scattered smaller mountain ranges, basins, valleys, and magnificent dunes. Hundreds of acres of these dunes are preserved

White sand dunes composed of mineral gypsum spread over vast regions of the Chihuahuan Desert in New Mexico.

in the White Sands National Monument, a 275-square-mile (712-sq-km) park at the New Mexico-Mexico border. These dunes are made of a powdery white mineral called gypsum. Rain has dissolved the gypsum out of the limestone rock in the surrounding mountains and carried it down the mountain to a playa on the basin floor. Strong winds have blown the gypsum across the basin and into dunes. The strong winds that began shaping the dunes millions of years ago still shape and reshape the dunes today.

These gypsum dunes don't stay put; they move constantly, as much as 40 feet (12 m) a year. This movement creates an extremely challenging environment for living things. Even plants and animals adapted to hot, dry desert conditions struggle to survive here. Nevertheless, a hundred different species of plants and animals can be found in the White Sands. Many have adapted to life in the dunes in some surprising and unusual ways.

The world's first atomic bomb was detonated in 1945 in New Mexico's White Sands region of the Chihuahuan Desert. Since 1951, more than 700 nuclear devices have been exploded in the Great Basin's Nevada Test Site.

Life exists in the dunes because there is water here. Even though the summer thunderstorms bring less than 10 inches (25 cm) of rain, sand dunes are some of the wettest places in the desert. Even in the driest season, if you poke your finger just a few inches into the gypsum sand you will feel moisture. This water is loosely held by the sand-sized gypsum particles. When it rains, because little runoff or erosion occurs, plants have a better chance of soaking up the water. In soils made of finer particles, such as clay, water is bound tightly to the soil and is more difficult for the plants to get. The sand is moist for other reasons, too. Microscopic organisms—bacteria and algae— live between the grains of sand near the surface. One variety of bacteria can absorb as much as ten times its weight in water. When the rain falls, these bacteria help the dunes act like giant sponges, absorbing and holding as much water as possible.

But plants cannot live on water alone. They also need nutrients, such as nitrogen, phosphorus, and potassium. In other environments, these nutrients come from organic matter in the soil. In the

The roots of plants such as the rosemary mint secure a place in the shifting sand by forming fortress-like mounds called pedestals.

gypsum dunes, most of the organic material dries up and is blown away by the wind. Most of the nutrients available to plants are provided by those same microscopic bacteria and algae that live in the top layer of sand. These **organisms**—living things—can take nitrogen out of the air and convert it into a form that plants use for photosynthesis. The bacteria and algae bind together with the sand particles and form a crust on top of the sand. This crust is described as **cryptobiotic**, meaning "hidden life," because the organisms that form it cannot be seen with the naked eye. The cryptobiotic crust helps stabilize the sand dunes by resisting wind and water erosion. These crusts are strong, but they are also very fragile. One footstep breaks the crust and greatly reduces the organisms' ability to provide water and nutrients to plants. A jeep or dune-buggy drive can damage the dunes and change them from a place where plants and animals can survive, to a place where they cannot. In the desert, the hidden life is often the hardest to protect.

Put Them on a Pedestal

Staying put is the biggest problem for plants in shifting sand. All plants get their start in the flat areas between the dunes and along the edge of the dune field. Here, the sand moves very slowly—inches, not feet, a year. Seeds of nearly fifty species of grasses, wildflowers, herbs, cactuses, and woody plants sprout and begin to grow. But eventually the dunes move and begin to bury them. Plants have no way to escape. Many of the plants are simply smothered by the buildup of gypsum sand on top of them and they die. Other plants try to hold onto part of the dune. The skunkbush sumac, Rio Grande cottonwood, and rosemary mint, for example, send their roots out and down to form a kind of cage around the sand. Within this cage of roots, the gypsum forms into a hard mound called a **pedestal**. As the sand shifts over them, these pedestals are left behind for the plants to continue growing in. Often pedestals formed by many different plants will merge together and create giant pedestals measuring 50 feet (15 m) high and 80 feet (24 m) in diameter. They become islands of stability in a sea of moving sand.

Pedestals show how living and nonliving things affect each other in the desert ecosystem. In response to shifting sand (a nonliving thing), plants (a living thing) grow a vast network of roots that form pedestals (another nonliving thing). These pedestals can be massive enough to deflect the wind (nonliving) and change its course. Behind the pedestals, in an area protected from the wind, the sand moves more slowly, and plants (more living things) have a better chance of taking root.

The soaptree yucca has developed remarkable adaptations that allow it to grow up with the dunes. When sand begins to rise up the yucca's trunk, it blocks the sunlight from part of the plant. The plant responds by growing very rapidly—as much as 12 inches (31 cm) a year. Within the dunes, soaptree yuccas may reach 30 feet (9 m); outside the dunes, they normally grow about half that tall. When you see a yucca plant on top of a sand dune, you can be sure that beneath it is a long stem that stretches all the way through the sand to where it first established its roots.

Disappearing Acts

Shifting sand is not a problem for animals in the dunes. They can escape by walking, crawling, slithering, flying, or hopping away. Animals have other things to escape: sun, heat, and predators. But where do they go in an open desert of pure white sand? Underground. Most animals who live in the dunes, from caterpillars to kit foxes, have the ability to dig burrows. They dig their burrows near the flat areas between the dunes or near plant communities at the edge. The burrows provide a cool, shaded home where the temperature is about 30 degrees Fahrenheit (17° C) cooler than the outside air. When summer daytime temperatures reach 100 degrees F (38° C), the burrows are a comfortable 70 degrees F (21° C). Because the sand is moist in the burrow, animals lose less water from their bodies through evaporation. Large animals, such as the coyote and kit fox, dig deep burrows in the sand. Smaller creatures, such as caterpillars and spiders, don't excavate permanent burrows, but they do crawl and hide just beneath the surface of the sand. Lizards and other patient predators track small moving ridges and bumps of sand across the desert. Just beneath the surface is their next meal—a moist, cool caterpillar or a spider.

Soaptree yuccas grow above the level of the sand to avoid being buried by it.

Pedestals are one of the favorite places for animals to burrow. The root-reinforced pedestals make a more solid, permanent burrow. They are also very convenient food sources. For the primary consumers, the plants growing in the pedestal provide blossoms, leaves, seeds, and fruit. For the predator, the pedestals are prime hunting grounds for insects and other small animals.

Many nocturnal desert animals, such as the kit fox, avoid extreme heat and most predators. But in the Chihuahuan's white sand dunes, nocturnal habits aren't always enough. Dark-colored animals are easily spotted against the white gypsum sand—even at night. For extra camouflage, some small animals, such as Apache pocket mice, snout beetles, Cowles prairie lizards, and bleached earless lizards have evolved a white coloration. Because this adaptive coloration is so specific to the gypsum dunes, some species are lighter in color than the same species living just a short distance from the dunes. And because light colors tend to reflect rather than absorb sunlight, this color adaptation also helps keep animals cooler.

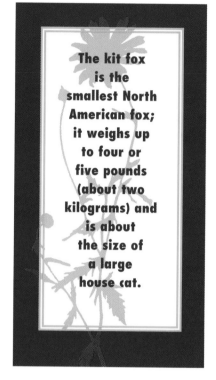

The kit fox is the smallest North American fox; it weighs up to four or five pounds (about two kilograms) and is about the size of a large house cat.

Aliens Invade!

The plant and animal communities at White Sands National Monument are facing new threats from the tamarisk and the oryx. The tamarisk is a plant native to North Africa, the Mediterranean, and the Middle East, where it grows as a woody shrub or small tree. It thrives in arid climates in nutrient-poor soil. Tamarisk grows along streams and springs, spreads quickly, and forms dense thickets. Starting in the 1850s, tamarisk was imported to the United States for use in erosion control throughout the Southwest. While the trees have helped control erosion, the tamarisk has spread to areas where it is extremely destructive. At White Sands tamarisk is called an invasive exotic because it is a non-native species that has invaded many of the flat areas between the dunes, where it threatens to choke out the native plants. Tamarisk builds the largest pedestals of any plant

Species such as the collared lizard have evolved a white coloration that helps camouflage them in the white dune environment.

in the dunes and can out-compete other plants for water. A single, large tamarisk can completely dry up a water source, absorbing up to 300 gallons (1,135 l) of water a day. In addition to choking out plants, the tamarisk is not a favorite food source for animals. At White Sands, ecologists are now studying ways to get rid of the tamarisk so that it doesn't completely displace the native species. Eradication is difficult because the tamarisk resprouts quickly after cutting or burning. Laws are being enacted to prevent these trees from being imported.

The oryx is a large African antelope that now lives in White Sands. Nearly one hundred oryx were brought here by the New Mexico Department of Game and Fish in the 1970s to establish a population of big game animals for sport hunting. There are now about one thousand oryx here. Unfortunately, the oryx devours plants, such as desert grasses and yucca. The National Park Service, which runs White Sands, is concerned about the impact of this non-native oryx on the desert ecosystem. A suggestion was made to introduce predatory mountain lions to reduce the oryx population. This solution was rejected because it would alter the food chain. If the food chain is altered, then the food web is affected. If the food web is affected, the entire ecosystem could change. To maintain the natural balance of the ecosystem within White Sands, the park service simply fenced the park boundary to keep the oryx out.

Shaped by Water

Deserts may get very little rain, but what they do get shapes the entire ecosystem—the landforms, the plant and animal communities, and their interactions. Even though the total amount of precipitation each year is small, less than 10 inches (25 cm) a year, the effect of this moisture over millions of years is enormous. In the deserts of the Colorado Plateau, the effect is mind-boggling. Water has carved the colorful rock layers into mile-deep canyons, massive free-standing arches, terraces, and shapes that look like fins, castles, thrones, chimneys, and tables. It is a landscape that seems possible only in our imaginations.

The desert of the Colorado Plateau spreads across Colorado, Utah, Arizona, and New Mexico. It is a desert of great depth and height—from canyon floors below sea level to mountain peaks towering 11,000 feet (3,355 m). These dramatically different elevations have produced a range of climates that are similar to icy polar tundra at the highest points and the hottest deserts at the lowest.

Through time, water has shaped the dramatic landforms that characterize the desert regions of the Colorado Plateau.

Because of these variations of temperature and elevation, water is present in the deserts of the Colorado Plateau as rain, snow, and ice. These three forms of water **weather**, or break down, rocks and **erode**, or wash away, the broken-down rock. Rock is weathered as small amounts of water seep into cracks. In winter, the water freezes, expands, and begins to push apart the rock. When the ice melts, the water further loosens the rock. Over time, the rock splits apart and is broken into smaller and smaller pieces. Once the rock is weathered, it is gradually eroded into a fine sediment, which washes quickly away.

In the deserts of the Colorado Plateau, the power of water to erode rock is greatest during the summer. Sudden and violent rainstorms, accompanied by thunder and lightning, unleash torrents of water. In a matter of minutes, several inches of rain may fall. Water gushes down the hills in broad flat sheets, then collects in small channels as it flows downhill. It turns thick and muddy as it erodes sand and clay from the hills. As the water picks up speed, it also picks up weathered rocks, which scrape, scour, and gouge the land. Dry stream beds, called washes, or **arroyos**, quickly turn into fast-moving streams that overflow and break their banks. Twenty-foot-high (6-m) walls of muddy water move down through the desert, sweeping up tons of sediment, rocks, and boulders, uprooting plants and trees, and drowning animals. Floodwater may lose power and volume as it spreads out over flatter land, or it may rush full force into a larger body of water, such as the Colorado or Green Rivers. In a flash, the flood has come and gone and changed the desert forever.

These floods are part of a "vicious cycle" in the desert ecosystem. Flash floods wash away the organic material that helps make soil. Because there is so little soil, there are relatively few plants. Without plants, there are no roots to hold the small rocks and soil together; the ground has no natural buffer from the full effects of the

The Havasupai people inhabited the Grand Canyon region in Arizona on and off for more than 4,000 years. They farmed the inner canyon in the summer. In the winter, they migrated to the canyon rims, where they could find better shelter, more firewood, and deer. Today, the Havasupai have moved to the water-rich western portions of the canyon.

Sudden and unpredictable, flash floods sweep across the desert landscape.

sun, wind, water, and extreme heat and cold; and there is very little organic material to help make soil.

A Race Against the Sun

At Arches National Park in Utah, eons of constant weathering and erosion by flash floods have created thousands of natural stone arches, towering spires, deeply cut canyons, colossal stone walls, and 200-foot (60-m) vertical rock slabs. In the park, flash floods have scoured out many large holes, called potholes, which make the ideal environment for one of the desert's most amazing dramas of adaptation. Spadefoot toads burrow deep in the fine sediment within these potholes. The toad's entire life cycle is timed to take advantage of the park's summer rainstorms. Within hours of a heavy rain, the nocturnal toads emerge from their underground burrows to search for a mate. The males move quickly to the rain-filled potholes. Instantly, the males begin their raucous breeding calls, which can be heard for miles across the desert. The females soon follow the call to the pothole. The amphibians mate, and the female lays her eggs. Provided the pools do not dry up, the eggs will hatch into tadpoles within twenty-four hours. In just two weeks, the tadpoles will grow into small toads that will hop out of the pothole to begin life on land. By comparison, some species of spadefoot toads in the Eastern Woodland ecosystem require several months to complete this part of their life cycle.

The new generation of adult spadefoot toads stays close to the site of the rain pools. To escape the midday heat, the toads use the hard, crescent-shaped spades on their hind feet to burrow in the sandy soil. Burrows can be as deep as 20 to 25 inches (51–64 cm). At the onset of drought, they burrow one last time and begin a period of hibernation that usually lasts nine to eleven months. To protect their delicate skin from drying out between storms, the spadefoot toads encase themselves in several dry, hard layers of skin that they have loosely shed from their bodies. When the summer rains beat on the dry ground above them, the toads awaken and begin the cycle anew.

Like the spadefoot toads, tiny kangaroo rats are a marvel of adaptation to the desert. They never drink water. They get tiny amounts of water from the seeds they eat. Kangaroo rats make water inside their bodies from these seeds as they convert them into energy. Kangaroo rats have the most efficient kidneys of all mammals, producing urine so concentrated it crystallizes when it passes from their bodies. Their droppings are nearly dry. During hot, dry periods, they stay cool in their underground burrows, which are covered loosely with soil.

People, however, are lured to the Colorado Plateau neither by the diminutive kangaroo rat nor the nocturnal spadefoot but by the

The life cycle of the spadefoot toad is closely timed to seasonal rains.

Kangaroo rats manufacture water in their bodies as they metabolize the dry seeds that make up most of their desert diet.

natural beauty of this most sparsely populated region. The Colorado Plateau contains our largest concentration of national parks. These parks—the Grand Canyon, Arches, Bryce Canyon, Zion, Petrified Forest, Mesa Verde, Capitol Reef, and Canyonlands—preserve not only the plant and wildlife communities but the archaeological remains of early Indian civilizations. More than five million people visit Grand Canyon National Park each year. Like many national parks, the Grand Canyon includes hotels, restaurants, visitors centers, parking lots, and campgrounds. These facilities make visits to the park more enjoyable for many people. But with the facilities and the millions of annual visitors come traffic, air pollution, an increasing need for water and electricity, and a diminished wildlife habitat.

To deal with these problems, the park establishes management plans, visitor policies, and rules and regulations for tour operators. The park service shoulders the responsibilty for balancing the often conflicting needs of visitors with the environment. To preserve the fragile and improbable worlds of the kangaroo rat, the spadefoot toad, and other life forms of the Colorado Plateau, the park urges visitors to "take only memories, leave only footprints."

Sagebrush, Salt, and Silver

There are deserts that visitors may only want to pass through—quickly—on their way to somewhere else. These deserts are massive expanses of flat land and uninviting mountains. The soil is poor. The vegetation is gray and scrubby. The hillsides are not full of colorful flowers or intriguing cactus shapes. In winter these deserts are bitter cold; in the summer they are broiling hot. Blizzards and drought are plentiful. In the Southwest, the Great Basin Desert is this kind of place. It blankets most of Nevada and parts of Oregon, Idaho, Utah, Wyoming, and California.

The Great Basin landscape is dominated by a series of long, narrow mountain ranges running north to south. Between the ranges lie vast shallow depressions called basins. Rivers, streams, runoff, and snowmelt in the mountains carry sediments and minerals down into these basins, but not out of them. Sediments build up on the basin floor. Once water is trapped in the basins, it can leave only through

The Great Basin is a cold desert. Summers are hot and dry, and winters are bitter cold and snowy.

evaporation. Heavy rains and spring runoff from snowy mountain ranges turn many of these basins into shallow, temporary lakes called **playas**. As the water in the playas evaporates, salt is leached from the soil, and the water left behind is very saline, or salty. In most cases it dries up completely, leaving a lake bed encrusted with saline residue. The combination of saline water and cold winters mean that many of the Southwest's hot-desert plant species cannot survive in the Great Basin. The saline soil would kill most plants and animals, and the spongelike trunks of the giant saguaro would freeze like popsicles in the winter. The Great Basin Desert is dominated by plants that can withstand all of these harsh conditions, or else avoid them.

The Sagebrush Story

Sagebrush is a kind of shrub, a woody, bushy plant that grows close to the ground. The Great Basin Desert is dominated by sagebrush—fourteen different species according to recent studies. Sagebrush is so hardy, so abundant here that this desert is nicknamed the Sagebrush Desert.

Sagebrush avoids the saline soil of the basins, but grows practically everywhere else. It prefers the lower slopes of the valleys between the mountain ranges.

Sagebrush is a keystone species of the Great Basin, much like the saguaro cactus of the Sonoran. Sagebrush plants provide shelter and food for many wildlife species. The names of many animals reveal their close connection to this plant: the sagebrush lizard, sagebrush chipmunk, sagebrush vole, sagebrush sparrow, and sage grouse. The animals in the sagebrush community use the plant in different ways, in different seasons, and at different times of the day. Many primary consumers live in, on, or under the sagebrush and rely on it for food. The pygmy rabbit, for instance, burrows at the base of the plant and nibbles its leaves. The turkey-sized sage grouse nests in the sagebrush and also hides from predators beneath its branches. The grouses feed on sagebrush buds and leaves. The sagebrush vole lives underground in colonies and eats its naturally shedding bark and twigs.

The Vanishing Playa

The desert landscape includes a great number of lakes. Most of them are shallow, temporary lakes, called playas, that form in flat-bottomed basins. Others, like the Great Salt Lake are shallow but hold water year-round. Desert lakes are extremely saline because they are fed by rainwater that dissolves and carries salts from the rocks in the surrounding mountains. As the water turns to vapor, the salt is left behind and accumulates in the lake bed. This experiment shows why desert lakes come and go so quickly and how salt builds up in the lake bed. You will need:

- a measuring cup
- a small bowl
- a large dinner plate, cookie sheet, or flat pan with low sides
- salt

1. Pour one cup (275 ml) of water into a small bowl. This is like a deep, freshwater lake with little surface area exposed to the air.

2. Add three tablespoons (45 ml) of salt to another cup (275 ml) of water. Stir to dissolve it completely. This gives the water about the same saltiness as the Great Salt Lake.

3. Pour the salty water onto a plate, cookie sheet, or flat pan. This is like the Great Salt Lake, or playa, with a large surface area exposed to the air.

4. Put the bowl and the plate side by side. Over several days you can watch the effects of evaporation. Weather permitting, put your two "lakes" outside; the sun, dry air, and wind will speed up the evaporation. Cover them up or bring them inside if it begins to rain or snow. During the winter, put your lakes indoors by a sunny window if possible.

5. In a few days, you'll notice that the level of the water in the bowl is a bit lower, but that the plate is completely dry. The plate will also be encrusted with salt left behind after the water was evaporated. In the desert, this salt builds up in the lake bed and discourages most plants from growing there.

6. Add enough water to the bowl and plate to return your lakes to their original level. Over the next week, replenish the water as the bowl and plate go dry. The shallow lake will need to be replenished many times before the bowl goes dry once.

With little precipitation, high evaporation rates, and lots of sunlight, do you think the desert playa will ever be permanent? What might happen if deep lakes in other ecosystems are gradually filled in by eroded sediments?

The hardy sagebrush provides food and shelter for many Great Basin animals, including the sage grouse.

The sagebrush community is an ideal place to see how closely life forms are connected in the desert. The sage thrasher, the sage sparrow, and the sagebrush lizard all live here. They are diurnal, so they need extra protection from predators. They have evolved the gray color of the sagebrush to help them hide in their host plants. The birds build well-camouflaged nests in the sagebrush by using fine shreds of the bark as nesting material. The lizard hunts for insects, scorpions, and snails in the open spaces among the sage-brush plants, then dashes for cover under the sagebrush when it is frightened. These animals have a mutualistic relationship with the sagebrush. While the sagebrush provides shelter and food, the insect-eating animals provide the sagebrush with pest control, and the seed-eating animals provide seed dispersal through their droppings.

The sagebrush also attracts other secondary consumers, such as the kit fox, bobcat, and coyote, which visit the plants to hunt for food. Because they hunt in the dark, these animals rely on their keen hearing rather than their eyes to detect their next meal. Larger mammals such as mule deer and pronghorn sheep may eat sage-brush as they browse through the desert. Cattle and sheep that graze in this habitat ignore the sagebrush but eat the grasses and other plants. This eliminates some of the sagebrush's competition and helps it thrive.

The Great Salt Lake

A few of the basins of the Great Basin Desert contain shallow permanent lakes. The largest and most famous of these is the Great Salt Lake in Utah. Rain and melted snow from the nearby Wasatch Mountains supply rivers that flow into the lake. Because the rate of evaporation is so high in the desert, great quantities of salt and other minerals are left behind as the water evaporates. The Great Salt Lake is eight times saltier than the ocean. Though too saline for fish, this lake supports nearly thirty different species of tiny plantlike organisms called algae. These algae, in turn, feed a large population of tiny brine shrimp and brine flies. In one section of the lake, a system of dikes separates the incoming fresh water from the salty water and has created a 400,000-acre (162,000-ha) freshwater marsh. A variety of freshwater aquatic insects live in the marsh. During the warmer months, millions of California gulls, white pelicans, blue herons, avocets, cormorants, ducks, and more than two hundred other species of birds stop here to feast on the shrimp, flies, and insects.

In the 1980s disaster struck the Great Salt Lake. Unusually heavy rain and snowfall in the Wasatch Mountains caused the level of the lake to rise 2 feet (.61 m) a year over several years. The salty water flooded the lands around the lake, threatening to destroy an ecosystem that included plant and animal communities as well as the human communities in nearby towns. By 1986, the level of the lake had risen 12 feet (3.6 m). The freshwater marshes were flooded with salty water, which destroyed plants such as cattails and rushes. All of the fish died, as did hundreds of thousands of birds who nested there. The advancing waters forced some shorebirds to rest on people's lawns. Migrating birds bypassed the lake, stopping instead at nearby freshwater marshes newly created from the heavy rains and melt. Tens of millions of dollars of homes, farms, crops, and property were destroyed. No one could predict when the flooding would stop. Something had to be done.

Wildlife experts, scientists, lawmakers, engineers, and conservationists came up with a plan. Three giant pumps were built on the shore of the Great Salt Lake. In 1987, they began pumping water out of the lake at the rate of 1.2 million gallons (4.5 million l) a minute.

For two years, water was pumped along a canal and onto a vast, salty area of open desert called a salt flat. On this nearly lifeless flat, the pumped water created a 500-square-mile (1,295-sq-km) pond that evaporated over a few years. Once the Great Salt Lake returned to its normal size, it took five years for the plant life to return to the marshes. It took another five for the migrating birds to come back.

The Great Basin Desert is rich not only in salt, but in other minerals such as gold and silver. About fifteen different kinds of salt, including table salt, are extracted from the lake. The water is pumped out of the lake and into evaporation ponds. When the water evaporates, the dry salts and minerals left behind are processed.

Other minerals are harder to extract. Since the discovery of gold in the West in the 1840s, fortune seekers from all over the world have flooded the Great Basin. Many were just passing through on their way to the gold mines of California. Countless other miners endured the desert's harsh climate to dig, pick, blast, crush, drill, and wash the gold, silver, and copper out of the rock deep beneath the surface of the ground. These mines have left scars on the desert—gaping mine shaft holes, pits the size of canyons, mining equipment, and massive piles of residue and leftover chemicals.

Containing both salt and fresh water, the Great Salt Lake supports hundreds of species of birds, such as this American avocet.

Minerals extracted from the Great Basin Desert include gold, silver, and salt.

Today, large mining companies are extracting more and more gold and silver from the Great Basin Desert. Nevada is the largest producer of these metals in the United States. But sagebrush may be more valuable than gold and silver: Scientists have recently discovered that as sagebrush plants draw up water and minerals from a vast area, they offer clues about the precious minerals that lie beneath them. Scientists can analyze the chemicals in the leaves to determine if there is gold or silver in the soil.

A Balancing Act

The Mojave Desert stretches across southern California and parts of Nevada and Arizona. The Mojave forms a transition zone between the Great Basin Desert to the north and the Sonoran Desert to the south. Parts of this desert resemble the basin-and-range, shrub-covered landscapes of the Great Basin, other parts look more Sonoran with bajadas washed in spring flowers. Many plants and animals of both the Sonoran and Great Basin Deserts live here. In addition, there are a number of species that live only in the Mojave, such as the Joshua tree, which reaches heights of 30 feet (9 m) and often forms small forests. The Joshua tree was named by nineteenth century pioneers who traveled across the desert looking for a place to settle. They believed the tree looked like the biblical leader Joshua praying with his arms upraised.

A traveler crossing the Mojave today would find the Joshua tree branches pointing in all directions toward major metropolitan areas slowly encroaching the once-uninhabitable desert lands. Los Angeles, San Bernadino, and their surrounding suburbs are sprawling from California in the southeast. In

Joshua trees create an otherworldly landscape in the Mojave Desert.

Nevada, the city of Las Vegas lights up the Mojave for miles around. Small towns are scattered all over the Mojave too. The impact of towns and cities on the desert is profound.

Life in the desert depends on water. When plants, animals, and people are in direct competition for this most precious resource, the ecosystem can become imbalanced. What we would consider a minor change in the water supply or quality of water can be critical, even fatal, to a plant or animal. In two very different regions of the Mojave in California, the ongoing struggle to maintain a balance has been acted out in some surprising ways.

Life in Death Valley

Few places in the Southwest desert capture the imagination like Death Valley. It is the desert pushed to extremes, one of the lowest, hottest, driest places on Earth. The valley's flat, salty floor is 282 feet (86 m) below sea level. The park gets just 1.6 inches (41 mm) of rain each year, and some years pass without a drop. The temperature in the shade has reached 134.6 degrees F (57° C); the ground temperature has soared to an impossible 201 degrees F (94° C). Normal summer air temperatures are a bit cooler—around 120 degrees F (48° C). The expected survival time for a person resting in the shade here during the summer is less than two days. Now *that's* a desert.

Even in this forbidding desert environment, hundreds of species of plants and animals survive quite well. The rare desert pupfish lives in the creeks, pools, and springs. An unlikely place for fish to be sure, but the two-inch-long (5-cm) pupfish has adapted to its environment in some unlikely ways. The pupfish community is a small one: they live on algae and a few insects and have no predators except possibly the great blue heron and the white-faced ibises. Pupfish are a very small link in a short food chain.

One species of pupfish lives in Salt Creek, which runs through the floor of Death Valley. Much of the creek dries up during the

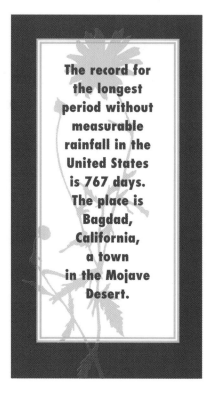

The record for the longest period without measurable rainfall in the United States is 767 days. The place is Bagdad, California, a town in the Mojave Desert.

summer, so the pupfish move into the deeper pools that remain. These pools get hot in the summer, but pupfish are among the most heat-tolerant of all fish. They have been known to survive in water as high as 112 degrees Fahrenheit (44° C). During the summer, the temperature of the Salt Creek pools regulary reaches over 100 degrees F (38° C). The pupfish dive down and burrow in the mud at the bottom of the pool. When the water cools down after dark, they swim back to the top. Pupfish are also salt tolerant. They can survive in water two to three times saltier than seawater. This is important because as the deeper pools evaporate in the summer, the dissolved salts become even more concentrated. Pupfish drink the salt water, then excrete excess salts through their kidneys and gills.

Devil's Hole pupfish live in emerald green water deep inside a cave in Death Valley. These tiny fish were once at the center of a controversy that ended up in the United States Supreme Court. Real estate and agricultural developers wanted to drill wells on land adjacent to Death Valley National Park. The wells would provide great quantities of groundwater for irrigating the future farmland. A conservation group argued that the wells would change the level of the water in Devil's Hole and so destroy the pupfish's habitat. In court, the developers, the conservationists, and the pupfish all won. The

The Devil's Hole pupfish lives in the creeks and springs that form naturally in the desert.

wells were drilled and land is being irrigated. The water level in Devil's Hole is officially monitored, though. If the water level drops, the pumping must stop. For now, the pupfish is alive and well in Death Valley.

In the drier parts of Death Valley, the food chains get longer, more complex, and a bit more unusual. Antlion beetles dig small cone-shaped holes in the sandy soil. They wait down inside the hole. When it detects an ant near the opening of the hole, the antlion kicks sand at the ant to knock it down into the trap. When an ant falls in, it cannot crawl out.

Ants, especially harvester ants, are also a favorite food of the horned lizard. Horned lizards hunt for anthills in the loose soils of Death Valley's rocky slopes. The harvest ant can inflict a painful sting or bite, but this doesn't bother the horned lizard, whose skin is tough and scaly. Many horned lizards have horn-like projections on their head, body, and tail to protect them from soft-mouthed predators, such as the coyote or kit fox. When not ant eating, horned lizards bask in the sun to warm up or seek a shady spot to cool down. Like all reptiles, they are cold-blooded. They do not make their own body heat, but gain heat from their environment.

A horned lizard makes a challenging meal for any predator, except one—the wily roadrunner. The road-runner's sharp, strong beak means it can make a quick meal of the horned lizard. This desert bird is a skillful hunter. Though it rarely flies, its sturdy legs and feet with claws in front and back help it run at speeds of up to 15 miles (24 km) an hour. Because of its great speed on the ground, it has no predators. The roadrun-ner gets nearly all of its water from its food. Aside from horned lizards, the roadrunner also feeds on insects, scorpions, and snakes. One of these snakes is the Mojave Desert sidewinder. The sidewinder can move at amazing speeds across the sand in a series of sideways S-bends. Only two parts of its body touch the ground at any one time, protecting it from the hot sand. No

As part of a California gold-mining scam, an elaborate mansion, a desert hideaway for a Chicago millionaire, was built in Death Valley in 1922. "Scotty's Castle" still stands, with its seven fireplaces, half-ton chandelier, and indoor waterfall.

matter how it moves, it is no match for the roadrunner, though, who will use its feet and sharp beak in a battle to the death.

Not only are roadrunners strong, they are clever and use many different hunting skills. Roadrunners are often seen watching the large glass windows of the Death Valley visitors' center building. They wait there until a smaller bird, confused by the reflection in the glass, flies into the window and is stunned. The roadrunner quickly picks up the fallen bird and runs off to enjoy its next meal.

Large mammals also make Death Valley their home. Desert bighorn sheep are most commonly found in the higher elevations of the mountains where the temperatures are cooler. These large, deer-sized mammals are well adapted to the dry climate. In the summer, they can go without drinking water for three to five days. In the winter, they need to drink every ten to fourteen days. In between, they get much of the water they need from the plants they eat. They move about in small bands of three to five, browsing on more than forty different kinds of plants. Bighorn sheep eat lightly so they don't uproot or otherwise damage the plants they rely on. And because they roam in small groups, they don't trample and destroy as much vegetation as a large herd of mammals would.

Unfortunately, native bighorn sheep have been driven from their habitat by large populations of feral burros. These burros are descendants of tamed burros that were brought by miners to the Death Valley area in the 1880s. The burros that escaped or were abandoned after the miners left turned wild again. Thousands of the wild burros now live in Death Valley. Unlike the bighorn, burros roam in large herds and trample vegetation, destroying the habitat of the native bighorn. They also discourage the shy bighorn from drinking at watering holes. Great numbers of sheep have died from starvation or dehydration. In efforts to restore the bighorn sheep

Bighorn sheep can go without drinking water for several days.

Permanent underground supplies of water rise to the surface to create oases where desert fan palm and a diverse biological community are found.

habitat, the burros are being removed from the park. At first, the burros were trapped and killed. Now they are trapped and transported to live elsewhere in California. Many burros are adopted by farmers who use them to protect their cattle and by families who tame them as outdoor pets.

Ahhh . . . the Oasis

Thirsty animals and desert explorers seek shade and water. After your tour of the Southwest deserts, you yearn for deep shade and lots of cool fresh water. You want an **oasis**. In the desert, an area made fertile by a permanent supply of fresh water is called an oasis. Oases don't exist in every desert. But in the southern Mojave, there are several in Joshua Tree National Park. They form here as rainwater soaks into the earth and collects in underground rivers, lakes, and springs. This water flows to the surface through cracks in the earth and forms small ponds or water holes.

In the dry, rocky landscape, the oases are easy to spot. They are marked by towering desert fan palms. Depending on the size of the oasis, the number of palms may vary from one to several hundred. The abundant and permanent supply of water enables the palms to grow throughout the year. They often reach heights of 50 feet (15 m). Through the blistering summer heat, the desert fan palm keeps its lush green crown. Thousands of tiny roots spread out around the base of the tree and form a dense mat on the ground. This covering prevents other plants from intruding and competing for the water supply.

The palms attract animals to the oasis. The old fronds of the palm hang down along the trunk, forming a kind of skirt that shades the trunk from the drying effects of sun and wind and gives shelter to animals and birds. Fan palms are also a food source in the oasis. The palm produces millions of tiny white flowers that provide nectar to a variety of insects. The abundant clusters of palm fruit attract many songbirds and small rodents. As these animals feed in the tops of the palms, they knock fruit to the ground where coyotes and foxes can reach them.

Prehistoric desert peoples were well aware of the permanent water found here. Many Native Americans lived at the palm oases year-round, or at least during the warmer seasons, eating the fruits of the palm and thatching the roofs and walls of their dwellings with its fronds.

Water, Water, Everywhere

More than 150 oases dot southern California and Mexico's Baja Peninsula. Wherever there is fresh water and lots of sunshine, plants, animals, and humans gather. In the 1870s and 1890s railroads brought waves of miners and cattle ranchers. There was plenty of sunshine for everyone, but a convenient supply of fresh water was limited. Wells were dug for each home and farm to tap into the supply of groundwater.

By the early 1900s, entire valleys in the Mojave Desert had been irrigated for large-scale farming. Irrigation and air conditioning have turned a desert of small natural oases into a land of big artificial ones.

Today, the lush towns and cities offer a nearly unlimited supply of fresh water. Water from the Colorado River supplies the thirsty resort towns of Palm Springs and Rancho Mirage. A 242-mile-long (389-km) aqueduct carries the river water used for irrigation and for swimming pools, golf courses, and artificial lakes, where posh hotels sit on man-made islands. Clearly, the scales are tipped toward the human population when it comes to the water supply. This imbalance may have devastating effects on the deserts of tomorrow.

In Palm Springs, irrigation and air conditioning have turned the desert into an environment of abundant water, cool air, swimming pools, well-watered lawns, and luxurious resorts.

Tomorrow's Deserts

The Southwest desert ecosystem is always changing. Until recently most of these changes have been slow. The landforms, soil, water, and climate of today's desert are the result of billions of years of change. Plants and animals too have evolved new forms and habits in response to their dynamic environment.

Today, changes are occurring much more quickly. In the last 150 years, people have brought enormous changes, with the amount of water as the most dramatic. Deserts are defined by their scanty amount of water— less than 10 inches (25 cm) a year. Each saguaro cactus, kit fox, kangaroo rat, sagebrush, and pupfish has evolved to live in this arid environment. If we increase the amount of water in the desert, we change the entire ecosystem. An irrigated desert is not a desert.

With water comes the possibility of life. With irrigation comes the reality of large-scale agriculture, large cities, increased population, and interstate highways. As the desert is altered to meet people's needs, the habitats of many animals are destroyed and their populations diminished. Cropland, housing developments, and highways mean less land for animals to use for hunting and foraging.

Hoover Dam, one of the highest concrete dams in the world, stands in the Black Canyon of the Colorado River.

Many people believe the desert to be a barren and lifeless place. They believe that because they cannot see the plants and animals, they do not exist. This way of thinking has damaged the fragile desert ecosystem. Millions of acres of the "barren" Southwest desert are used by the armed forces for testing bombs and missiles. Huge craters from exploded bombs pock the earth and will never heal. Radiation and other chemicals from their first atomic bomb still linger in the ground at some sites.

Many desert areas, especially sand dunes, are permanently damaged from their use as public recreation sites. Thousands of people enjoy driving dune buggies and trail bikes through these areas. Desert soils damage easily; tracks and ruts caused by the big tires of an off-highway vehicle may last a century or more. And hydroelectric dams along the Colorado River have changed the power of this desert-sculpting river.

The management of the desert ecosystem requires teams of experts. Botanists study the plants of the desert, native and alien alike. They learn about the ways plants adapt to changes in the air, water, and soil. They also study the plants that Native Americans traditionally used for medicine, food, shelter, and clothing. Wildlife managers care for the populations of animals, such as bighorn sheep, burros, kit foxes, coyotes, oryx, and pupfish. They must decide when there are too few or too many of each species. Wildlife managers look for ways to reduce certain populations through hunting or trapping and relocating. Conservation biologists look after species that are rare, such as the Devil's Hole pupfish. Restoration ecologists replant abandoned roads, old mining sites, and areas trampled by grazing animals and crowds of summer tourists.

Even if we do not live near the desert, our lives are affected by it. Although the irrigation of desert valleys in southern California increases the supply and variety of food at our grocery store, many experts fear that the irrigation will deplete underground water and reduce soil fertility by depositing salts on the land. The damming of the Colorado River helps bring electricity to homes outside the Mojave Desert. But because the dam restricts the flow of the Colorado, it has caused the level of the river to drop and eliminated the scouring floodwaters. The riverbanks and beaches are now over-crowded with new plants and shrubs. The cold, deep waters of the lakes formed by the dams have eliminated three species of native fish that lived in the warmer waters of the Colorado River. Although the hamburgers we eat for lunch may be from cattle grazing on grasses planted in the Great Basin Desert, the cattle and grasses form links in a new food chain that may eventually alter the entire ecosystem. We love to tour the national parks of the Southwest in our cars and campers, but this reduces animal habitats, which are paved over to build roads and parking lots.

So much of desert life is nocturnal, camouflaged, migratory, stored in seeds, hiding in burrows, or hidden in the crust of the sand. We must be patient observers and careful explorers in the ecosystem. Helping to restore the desert means understanding that we are connected to this place of abundant life.

Although the desert environment is a harsh one, the life forms, such as the saguaro's flowers, within it are surprisingly delicate and fragile.

Glossary

adaptation the special features and tricks developed by organisms to help them survive in a particular environment. The white coloration of the Apache pocket mouse is an adaptation that allows it to be camouflaged against the white sand in which it lives.

annual a plant that completes its entire life cycle in a short time, usually within one season. Annuals cannot withstand the seasons of drought and heat.

arroyo a normally dry streambed that has water in it periodically, usually after heavy rains.

bajada a gently sloping hill made of gravel, sand, and silt, washed down from the surrounding mountains.

biodiversity the variety of plant and animal species in an area.

biological community all of the organisms that live together and interact in a particular environment.

cryptobiotic means "hidden life"; cryptobiotic soil crust, for example, is formed by living organisms that are hidden, or not visible to the naked eye.

decomposer an organism that gets its energy by breaking down dead organisms (i.e., by rotting them). Fungi and many types of bacteria are decomposers that feed on dead plants and animals.

diurnal active during the day.

ecologist a scientist who studies the relationships among species and their environment.

ecosystem the association of living things in a biological community, plus its interaction with the nonliving parts of the environment.

environment all the living and nonliving things that surround an organism and affect its life.

erode to wash away material that has been weathered by sun, water, or wind.

food chain a feeding relationship in which one organism is eaten by another organism, which is in turn eaten by a larger organism.

food web the interaction among all the food chains.

habitat the place that has all the living and nonliving things that an organism needs to live and grow.

keystone species a species that has a large effect on many species in its community or ecosystem. The saguaro cactus is a keystone species because it affects many other species, such as woodpeckers, owls, and mice, which use the cactus as a food source or nesting site.

mutualistic the nature of a relationship between organisms in which both benefit. The gila woodpecker and the saguaro cactus have a mutualistic relationship; the saguaro provides a cool, well-protected nesting site for the woodpecker, and the woodpecker eats potentially damaging insects off the cactus.

nocturnal active during the night.

oasis an area in the desert made fertile by a permanent supply of fresh water.

organic matter decayed plants and animals.

organism a living thing, such as a plant or animal.

pedestal a hard mound of sand formed by the root system of a plant. In a sand dune, the pedestal remains while the looser sand around it is blown away.

perennial a plant that can withstand periods of drought and heat and live during all seasons of the year for several years.

photosynthesis the process by which plants and some other organisms that have chlorophyll use sunlight, carbon dioxide, and water to make sugars and other substances.

playa a shallow, temporary lake often located in a basin.

predator an animal that hunts or kills other animals for food. A kit fox that eats mice is a predator. Predators are also called **secondary consumers**.

primary consumer an animal that eats plants. The kangaroo rat is a primary consumer because its diet consists only of plants.

producer an organism (generally a plant) that converts solar energy to chemical energy by photosynthesis.

vapor tiny droplets of water suspended in the air. Vapor in the air makes it feel humid outside.

water cycle the process by which water is transformed from vapor in the atmosphere to precipitation upon land and water surfaces and ultimately back into the atmosphere.

weathering the process by which rocks are broken down into smaller and smaller pieces.

Further Exploration

Books

Arnold, Caroline. *Watching Desert Wildlife*. Minneapolis, MN: Carolrhoda Books, Inc., 1993.

Arritt, Susan. *The Living Earth Book of Deserts*. Pleasantville, NY: Reader's Digest, 1993.

Larson, Peggy. *The Sierra Club Naturalist's Guide to the Deserts of the Southwest*. Tucson, AZ: Southwest Parks and Monument Association, 1985.

Lerner, Carol. *A Desert Year*. New York: Morrow Junior Books, 1991.

MacMahon, James A. *The Audubon Society Nature Guides: Deserts*. New York: Alfred A. Knopf, 1985.

Savage, Stephen. *Animals of the Desert*. Austin, TX: Raintree Steck-Vaughn, 1997.

Sayer, April Pulley. *Desert*. New York: Twenty-First Century Books, 1994.

Weiwandt, Thomas A. *The Hidden Life of the Desert*. New York: Crown, 1990.

Organizations

Arches National Park, P.O. Box 907, Moab, UT 84532; (801) 259-8161.

Death Valley National Park, Death Valley, CA 92328; (760) 786-2331.

Joshua Tree National Park, 74485 National Park, Dr., Twentynine Palms, CA 92277; (760) 367-5500.

Organ Pipe Cactus National Monument, Route 1, Box 100, Ajo, AZ 85321; (520) 387-6849.

Southwest Parks and Monuments Association, 221 N. Court St. Tucson, AZ 85701; (520) 622-1999.

Utah Division of Wildlife Resources, 1594 West Temple, Salt Lake City, UT 84110; (801) 538-4700. Request a copy of "The Great Salt Lake: Utah's Amazing Inland Sea."

White Sands National Monument, P.O. Box 1086, Holloman AFB, NM 88330; (505) 479-6124.

Index

Page numbers for illustrations are in **boldface**.

$27.07

DATE			